HAGGY DOG BOOKS

STR BUT RUE

Compiled by De-ann Black
Illustrated by Mike Phillips

INDEX
BOOKS LTD

This edition published 2006 for Index Books Ltd.
Henson Way, Kettering, Northants, NN16 8PX

Contents

Introduction

People do the strangest things – most of them don't even realise how dumb they are! This book is filled with real-life humour, unintentional gaffes, stupid quotes, hilarious misprints and bizarre behaviour.

From weird news and crazy advertisements, to ridiculous fast-food fiascos and oddball tales, this book is packed with some of the silliest things to have happened.

. . .and the strangest thing is, they're all genuine!

Mobile bum

An American attorney had to have a mobile phone removed from his bum.

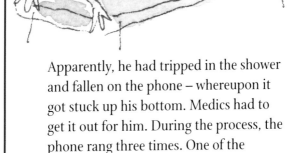

Apparently, he had tripped in the shower and fallen on the phone – whereupon it got stuck up his bottom. Medics had to get it out for him. During the process, the phone rang three times. One of the doctors commented that they had all joked about the incident (including the attorney), saying that by the time they finished, they had expected to find an answering machine up there too. Had the man been able to answer his phone calls, it would have given a whole new meaning to the light-hearted phrase that lawyers 'talk out of their arses'.

Out of court

Two clients were advised by their lawyers to settle their business argument out of court because it would be cheaper. The clients agreed. Later, the two men arranged to meet and beat each other up. Passers-by saw the fight, called the police, and both men were arrested and fined.

Law suits

The Law Society in America advised lawyers not to wear pinstripe suits or polka dot ties, as it makes them look untrustworthy. (You think?)

Apple Corporation sues itself

Industrial analysts were puzzled when Apple Computers filed a lawsuit against Apple Computers Corporation. (In other words, Apple were suing themselves.) The company claimed that Apple had violated the look and feel of the machines that had helped to make the company famous. An Apple spokesperson stated: "This is no joke. If we don't protect our copyrighted interface, everyone will use it and we could lose the exclusive right. So it is in our best interests to sue anyone who uses the Macintosh look and feel, including ourselves."

On the run

A lawyer asked the judge to reduce his client's bail as there was no risk that he would flee.

Just then, the client ran from the courtroom and out the front door. He was captured by police and taken back to the courtroom where his bail was increased.

Stupid bluff

A drunk robber threatened to 'call the police' if two petrol station attendants didn't hand over the money from the cash register. When the attendants refused, the robber called his own bluff and phoned the police – who arrested him!

Drop the salami

German police responded to a call from a man who thought he saw three men in a car struggling with a gun. When the police approached the vehicle, they found the 'gun' was a large sausage. The men were having a snack and passing the sausage around so they could all have a bite.

Salami whammy

A man attempted to rob a delicatessen in Miami, but he was attacked by the owner who whacked him with a giant salami.

It just wasn't the thief's day, because when he ran away from a further battering, he hid in the boot of a car parked nearby. Unknown to him, the car had undercover police officers in it!

Misquoted

Police in Los Angeles were successful with a robbery suspect who couldn't control himself during a line-up. When detectives asked each man in the line-up to repeat the words: "Give me all your money or I'll shoot", the man shouted, "That's not what I said!"

Non-lethal weapon

A man was arrested in California for trying to hold up a Bank of America branch without a weapon.

He used his thumb and finger to simulate a gun, but unfortunately, he forgot to keep his hand in his pocket.

What was he thinking?

A man from Illinois, pretending to have a gun, kidnapped a motorist and forced him to drive to two different cashpoint machines. The kidnapper proceeded to withdraw money from his own bank accounts!

Work for your money

A man walked into a Kansas Kwik Stop and demanded all the money in the cash drawer.

Allegedly, there wasn't a lot of money, so the thief tied up the store clerk and worked the counter himself for three hours until the police showed up and arrested him.

Smash bang

A man decided to smash an off-licence window to steal some beer. He thought he'd throw a brick through it and grab some booze.

Unfortunately, when he threw the brick at the window, it bounced back and knocked him unconscious. It seems the off-licence windows were made of Plexiglas™ – and the attempted smash and grab was caught on videotape.

Under-age thinking

A young man robbed a store with a shotgun, and demanded all the money from the cash drawer. The cashier put it in a bag. Then the robber saw a bottle of Scotch and told the cashier to put it in the bag as well.

The cashier refused, saying: "I don't believe you're over 21". The robber said he was, but the clerk still didn't believe him. At this point the robber took his driver's licence out of his wallet and showed it as proof. The cashier looked it over, and agreed that the man was in fact over 21 and put the Scotch in the bag. The robber then ran from the store with his loot. The cashier promptly called the police and gave them the name and address of the robber, as detailed on the licence. The police arrested the robber two hours later.

Bandits

Two Michigan robbers entered a record shop nervously waving revolvers. The first one shouted: "Nobody move!" When his accomplice moved, the startled first bandit shot him.

This iz a stikkup

A man walked into a Bank of America in San Francisco and wrote on a deposit slip, "This iz a stickup. Put all your muny in this bag".
While waiting in line to give his note to the cashier, he began to worry that someone had seen him write the note and might call the police. So he left the Bank of America and crossed the street to Wells Fargo. Here, he handed his note to the Wells Fargo cashier. She read it and, surmising from his spelling errors that he wasn't the brightest light, told him that she could not accept his stick-up note because it was written on a Bank of America deposit slip and that he would either have to fill out a Wells Fargo deposit

slip or go back to the Bank of America. Looking somewhat defeated, the man said, "Okay", and left. He was arrested a few minutes later waiting in line at the Bank of America.

Speed trap

A motorist was caught in an automated speed trap that measured his speed using radar and photographed his car.

He later received a ticket fine for $40 in the post. Thinking he was smart, the man sent the police department a photograph of $40. Days later, he received a letter from the police containing a picture of a pair of handcuffs. He immediately posted the $40 fine.

Bouncers

Two armed men rushed the front door of First American Bank just after the manager opened up.

Unknown to the men, the door had locked behind the manager and was firmly shut. The first robber bounced off the door hitting the second man. They managed to escape in their van and have not been captured.

Film star

A robber had the sense to disable a video surveillance camera during a break-in and took the camera with him as he fled. However, he didn't have the sense to take the recorder to which the camera was connected. Police found a full facial shot of him on tape reaching for the camera.

Sly detector

Police in Pennsylvania interrogated a suspect by placing a metal colander on his head and connecting it with wires to a photocopier. The message 'He's lying' was in the copier, and police pressed the copy button each time they thought the suspect was lying. The suspect believed the 'lie detector' was working and confessed everything.

FBI forgot about thief

FBI and Florida state authorities arrested a man who had been sentenced to five years in prison (twelve years earlier) for grand theft. The man had never been jailed. After the trial, he had gone home from the sentencing hearing, and 'sat tight' as suggested by his lawyer, waiting for notification to report to prison. Authorities forgot about him for twelve years!

Teen scene

Four teenagers were arrested in the parking lot of a large shopping centre in Lakeland, Florida. They had attempted to steal a random vehicle, but had broken into a police van containing three officers on a stakeout.

Nabbed by his mum

In Italy, a man suspected of snatching handbags was arrested by the police after he was reported by his mum! Unfortunately, while he was on his high-speed motorcycle snatching women's bags, he stole his mother's purse. He hadn't recognised her – but she recognised him!

Head bangers

Police arrested two men for fighting and took them to hospital for treatment for injuries to their heads. The police charged them with disorderly conduct and disturbing the peace, but not assault. It seems that the men were trying to prove who was more drunk by bashing their heads into the doors and walls of their apartment. They had, therefore, each injured themselves and not each other.

Chess-hire cat

A man was trying to teach his cat to play chess. His friend was astonished and asked: "Why are you trying to teach the cat to play chess?" The owner replied: "Because he couldn't pick up backgammon."

Holiday on Uranus

Con men obtained money from people by advertising holidays in space.
They had a brochure of the places you could visit including Mars, Venus, the Moon and Uranus. In the brochure it read: 'For the experience of a lifetime, look up Uranus'.

How far?

A holiday brochure feature stated: 'Relax in a Spanish vanilla. The fiesta has beautiful views and a slimming pool. Far hire is available as part of the deal – unlimited mileage'.

Brochure gaffe

A hotel brochure in Spain advertised – Romantic Rearends in a holiday resort.

Hotel rage

A guest who argued with a hotel receptionist had a bill pushed under his door. It was addressed to Mr B*****d.

Bargain deal

An extra bargain was on offer in a travel brochure: 'Every holiday to France comes with free children. Take home duty free'.

Love your bum

A survey by a toilet paper maker found that not many Britons loved their rear-ends.

Said a company spokesperson: "...just seven per cent of the nation currently love their bum. But those who do value their bottom seem to be male."

Quick nap

A Japanese bullet-train driver fell asleep for about eight minutes at the controls of one of the country's high-speed trains.

West Japan Railways said the train may have been travelling at up to 168 miles per hour. No one was hurt because the automatic control system took over and brought the train to a halt at the next station. This brings a whole new meaning to the phrase 'a quick nap'.

Shopaholics

Shopaholics are suffering from what is clinically known as 'oniomania'. This particular mania was identified 100 years ago by a German psychiatrist. When a female sufferer heard that there was a possible cure (a pill to sort out brain functions) she went on a shopping spree to celebrate.

Brussels prostitutes

This Government quote appeared in a national newspaper: 'The money will not be going directly into the prostitutes' pockets, but will be used to encourage them to lead a better life. We will be training them for new positions in hotels'.

Salami knickers

In a city's evening paper it stated:
'Police revealed that a woman arrested for shoplifting had a whole salami in her knickers. When asked why, she said it was because she was missing her Italian boyfriend.'

Gas gaffe

A national newspaper report: Commenting on a complaint from a Mr Arthur Purdey about a large gas bill, a spokesman for North West Gas said: "We agree it was rather high for the time of year. It's possible Mr Purdey has been charged for the gas used up during the explosion that destroyed his house".

Irish news

The following statement was issued by the Irish postal service to newspapers about their improved service.
'The mail used to be handled by hand, but now it's handled manually'.

Singing sandwich

A supermarket launched a musical Christmas sandwich. It played seasonal tunes like 'Jingle Bells'.

A sensor in the packet activated a small music box with a microchip. Sounds as good as it tastes!

German art

A man in Germany was wedged in the cat flap of his house for two days (before police rescued him) because passers-by thought he was a piece of 'installation art'. The man had lost his house keys and was using the cat flap to gain entry when he got stuck. Prankster students didn't help – they pulled his trousers and underpants down exposing his buttocks and erected a sign urging people to give money towards the 'street art' project. People assumed the man's screams for help were part of the performance and threw coins at him!

Mad margarine

Attention-seeking, ego-mad margarine has been designed for supermarkets in America. The margarine tubs shout and wiggle at customers – probably to butter them up!

Dodgy doughnuts

Austrian police raided bakeries across the country after a dodgy doughnut tip-off. They were informed that the doughnuts did not contain enough jam. A spokesman for the German press agency DPA said: "In every third doughnut tested by police food inspectors, the jam content was less than the prescribed 15 per cent."

There can be only one

A Spanish debt collector has started wearing a kilt to terrify people into paying up.

The man dresses in full Highland gear, including a hat and makeshift sporran, and is known as El Cobrador Escoses – the Scottish debt collector. Apparently the kilt works well because 'the Scots have a reputation for being very serious people, who are also sometimes aggressive'.

Clueless

An Aberdeen newspaper report stated that: 'At the height of the gale, the harbour master radioed a coastguard on the spot and asked him to estimate the wind speed. He replied that he was sorry, but he didn't have a gauge. However, if it was any help, the wind had just blown his Land Rover off the cliff'.

Marriage service

Customers waiting for car repairs in a garage in the US are offered a free marriage ceremony while they wait. The marriage deal is given with any 30,000-mile inspection of selected cars. For the price of the inspection, the garage owner will throw in the cost of being married by the local justice of the peace. The inspection comes with a warranty, but there is no guarantee on the marriage.

Weight watchers

Two skinny men seen stealing weights from a gym tried to carry them to their car. The weights were too heavy for the men, and one of them put his back out as he struggled with giant dumb-bells. His accomplice had to abandon the weights to drag his friend to the car. Both men drove off, leaving the weights behind.

No weather

A weather centre reported that there would be 'no weather' for the next two days because their monitoring equipment had been blown down during a storm – though they hazarded a guess that it would be windy!

Potty

A Potty Pageant in Santa Fe is being planned – and hopes to be launched in a huge splash of publicity. Over 200 toilets will be decorated and auctioned off. Everyone is encouraged to participate so that this plan doesn't go down the drain.

Ouch!

A man's car broke down in a car park, so he told his wife to go shopping in the nearby shopping centre while he fixed it.

She left him to sort the repair. The last thing she saw was her husband sliding under the rear end of the car with a toolbox. It was a warm summer's day and he was wearing baggy shorts. When she came back later, she noticed a crowd had gathered in the car park and people were giggling and pointing at her husband who was still lying under the car. His testicles were on display because his baggy shorts weren't covering him – and he'd no underpants on. She hurried over, stuck her hands up his shorts and arranged his testicles securely. When she had finished, she noticed that her husband was standing watching her from the other side of the car. Apparently, he'd asked a mechanic to help fix the car! The mechanic needed two stitches in his head.

Magic toilet

A hook-like device, called a Courtesy Wand, has been designed by an inventor in Georgia. It lets women lower the toilet seat without having to touch the pan. It's ideal for women whose men continually leave the seat up. At least someone's got a handle on the problem.

On your bike!

City officials in Santa Rosa, California, are encouraging commuters to use a non-polluting way of getting to work. They are offering free movie tickets as an incentive. The city's transit co-ordinator logs all the days people use alternative transport (bicycle, skateboard, running) and gives them the movie tickets. (Wonder if it's a drive-in movie?)

Saved by TV

A 71-year-old man fell off a dock into the jaws of an alligator – and survived because he knew how to defend himself against such an attack.

The man said: "I wasn't a bit afraid. I knew what they usually do". He'd been a fan of wildlife television programmes for years, and got away from the alligator by jabbing his thumb in its eye!

Jedi force

When filling in a 2001 census form, almost 400,000 Britons wrote that their religion was – 'Jedi'. This was in devotion to the *Star Wars* film series. May the force be with them.

Caught by the balls

A house-proud man was vacuuming when disaster struck – or rather, sucked! He was wearing only a dressing gown when it fell open, exposing his genitals. Bending over to cover himself, he accidentally put the vacuum cleaner too close to his scrotum – and it grabbed him by the balls. His testicles were torn and tattered, and although he's fine now, he'll be keeping the vacuum away from his manhood – and won't be a sucker again.

Repeated assault

Millions of Canadian office workers assault photocopiers.

A survey showed that the 'copy brats' kick and punch the photocopiers. (They should try pressing the buttons.)

Christmas cards

An Irish post office claimed that the reason millions of Christmas cards were delivered late was because many of them were the wrong shape.

Hop loader

A German priest has turned his 35-year-old washing machine into a fantastic new brewing device. He makes beer in his toploader, using it to heat and stir the mix. He washes his clothes in another machine now.

Anti-theft

An anti-theft device came in useful when a woman who was trying to secure it to the steering wheel of her car was attacked by a man. She used it to hit him over the head! Police later arrested the stunned attacker.

Tooth and claw

A newspaper reported that a young girl was blown out to sea on a set of inflatable teeth.

She was rescued by a man on an inflatable lobster. A coastguard spokesman commented: "This sort of thing is all too common these days".

Wrong gear

Four young men, dressed head to toe in Reebok and Nike sports gear, went into a gym in Scotland and asked the head female instructor about membership.

She offered them a 'free trial' of the gym equipment right there and then, but the men said they'd come back later because: "We haven't got our training gear on."

Macho elf

A nightclub security guard refused to dress up as one of Santa's elves at Christmas because: "…elves are just big fairies". The bouncer was, however, happy to dress up as a snowman because: "Frosty the Snowman's cool – and he's got a big hooter – the women will love it".

Dumb Laws

In California women may not drive in a house coat.

A law in Florida states that women may be fined for falling asleep under a hair dryer, as can the salon owner.

In Switzerland it is illegal to flush the toilet in an apartment after 10 pm. Also, a man may not relieve himself whilst standing up after 10 pm.

In Utah you may not cause a catastrophe and you must drink milk. The state also holds a husband responsible for every criminal act committed by his wife while she is in his presence.

Women must obtain permission from their husbands to wear false teeth in Vermont and neither sex may whistle underwater.

There are laws in Texas making it illegal to dust any public building with a feather duster, to possess realistic dildos or to land an aeroplane on the beach. You should also be careful not to take more than three swallows of beer while standing.

In the wilds of Alaska it is considered an offence to throw a live moose from a moving aeroplane or to wake a sleeping bear for the purposes of taking a photograph.

In some parts of Lousiana it is illegal to gargle in public. In other parts you may not tie an alligator to a fire hydrant.

Computer Chaos

A computer didn't work because the technician had forgotten to put in the memory chip.

Computer technician explains computer fault: "Without being too technical – it's f**d."**

Warning on computer: Keyboard not detected. Press F1 to continue.

A man phoned a computer advice line to ask where the 'space bar' was. They told him where it was on the keyboard. The following week, he phoned again for advice, apologising for being brainless. The instructor said: "Hey, there are some people who know less than you. Last week some idiot didn't even know where the space bar was".

A confused caller phoned IBM and said he was having trouble printing documents. He told the technical advisor that the computer had said it 'couldn't find the printer'. The user had also tried turning the computer screen to face the printer, but the computer still couldn't 'see' the printer.

Sign on the window of a computer shop: 'Out to Lunch. If not back by five, out for Dinner too.'

Essay Gaffes

Her vocabulary was as bad as, like, whatever.

It came down the stairs looking very much like something no one had ever seen before.

Her hair glistened in the rain like nose hair after a sneeze.

Her face was a perfect oval, like a circle that had its two other sides gently compressed by a Thigh Master.

She caught your eye like one of those pointy hook latches that used to dangle from doors and would fly up whenever you banged the door open again.

His thoughts tumbled in his head, making and breaking alliances like underpants in a tumble dryer.

The little boat gently drifted across the pond exactly the way a bowling ball wouldn't.

He was as lame as a duck. Not the metaphorical lame duck either, but a real duck that was actually lame. Maybe from stepping on a land mine or something.

It hurt the way your tongue hurts after you accidentally staple it to the wall.

The politician was gone but unnoticed, like the full stop after the Dr. on a Dr Pepper can.

Shots rang out, as shots are wont to do.

The young fighter had a hungry look, the kind you get from not eating for a while.

"Oh, Jason, take me!" she panted, her breasts heaving like a student on 31p-a-pint night.

John and Mary had never met. They were like two hummingbirds who had also never met.

The thunder was ominous sounding, much like the sound of a thin sheet of metal being shaken backstage during the storm scene in a play.

Long separated by cruel fate, the star-crossed lovers raced across the grassy field toward each other like two freight trains, one having left York at 6:36 pm travelling at 55 mph, the other from Peterborough at 4:19 pm at a speed of 35 mph.

The hailstones leaped from the pavement, just like maggots when you fry them in hot fat.

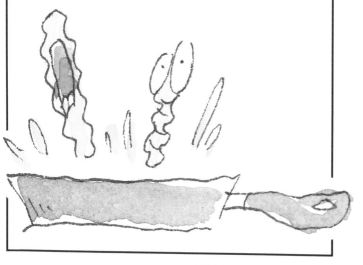

He was as tall as a six-foot-three-inch tree.

Even in his last years, Grandad had a mind like a steel trap, only one that had been left out so long it had rusted shut.

Her artistic sense was exquisitely refined, like someone who can tell butter from 'I Can't Believe It's Not Butter'.

She was as easy as the *Daily Star* crossword.

She walked into the office like a centipede with 98 missing legs.

Her voice had that tense, grating quality, like a first-generation thermal paper fax machine that needed a band tightened.

The revelation that his marriage of 30 years had disintegrated because of his wife's infidelity came as a rude shock, like a surcharge at a formerly surcharge-free cashpoint.

He was star-struck, as if a glittering star decoration had hit him on the head.

The ballerina rose gracefully en pointe and extended one slender leg behind her, like a dog at a lamppost.

Sports Quotes

"I know what is around the corner. I just don't know where the corner is" – Kevin Keegan

"England have the best fans in the world and Scotland's fans are second to none" – Kevin Keegan

"Chile have three options – they could win or they could lose" – Kevin Keegan

"It's like a toaster, the ref's shirt pocket. Every time there's a tackle, up pops a yellow card. I'm talking metaphysically now of course" – Kevin Keegan

"If history repeats itself, I should think we can expect the same thing again" – Terry Venables

"I would not be bothered if we lost every game as long as we won the League" – Mark Viduka

"When you get to the point where you don't believe you can win, there is no point in getting out of bed at the end of the day" – Stan Collymore

"I've had 14 bookings this season – eight of which were my fault, but seven of which were disputable" – Paul Gascoigne

"I've never wanted to leave. I'm here for the rest of my life, and hopefully after that as well" – Alan Shearer

"I'd like to play for an Italian club, like Barcelona" – Mark Draper

"You've got to believe that you're going to win, and I believe we'll win the World Cup until the final whistle blows and we're knocked out" – Peter Shilton

"I faxed a transfer request to the club at the beginning of the week, but let me state that I don't want to leave Leicester" – Stan Collymore

"Leeds is a great club and it's been my home for years, even though I live in Middlesbrough" – Jonathan Woodgate

"I couldn't settle in Italy – it was like living in a foreign country" – Ian Rush

"I always used to put my right boot on first, and then obviously my right sock" – Barry Venison

"The Brazilians were South American, and the Ukrainians will be more European" – Phil Neville

"Germany are a very difficult team to play… they had eleven internationals out there today" – Anonymous

"I'd rather play in front of a full house than an empty crowd" – Johnny Giles

"I took a whack on my left ankle, but something told me it was my right knee" – Lee Hendrie

"Football means more to me than others, though it is not less than they think I mean because I mean it" – Anonymous footballer

"Strangely, in slow-motion replay, the ball seems to hang in the air for even longer" – Anonymous football commentator

"Julian Dicks is everywhere. It's like they've got eleven Dicks on the field" – Football commentator

"What will you do when you leave football, Jack? Will you stay in football?" – Stuart Hall

"Ah, isn't that nice. The wife of the Cambridge president is kissing the cox of the Oxford crew" – Harry Carpenter's quote at an Oxford–Cambridge boat race

"This is a really lovely horse. I once rode her mother" – Horse racing commentator

"The lead car is absolutely unique, except for the one behind it which is identical" – F1 racing commentator

"And this is Gregoriava from Bulgaria. I saw her snatch this morning and it was amazing!" – Weightlifting commentator

"For those of you who are watching in black and white, the blue is behind the brown" – Snooker commentator

"And there goes Juantorena down the back straight, opening his legs and showing his class" – David Coleman at the Montreal Olympics

"One of the reasons Arnie (Arnold Palmer) is playing so well is that, before each tee shot, his wife takes out his balls and kisses them... Oh my God! What have I just said?!!!" – Golf commentator

"I've been boxing for eleven years. It's time I threw out my towel" – Anonymous boxer

Announcements on the London Underground

"Please mind the closing doors..." The doors close... The doors open. "Passengers are reminded that the big red slidey things on the side of the train are called the doors. Let's try it again, shall we? Please stand clear of the doors." The doors close... "Thank you."

"Ladies and Gentlemen, upon departing the train may I remind you to take your rubbish with you. Despite the fact that you are in something that is metal, fairly round, filthy and smells, this is a tube train for public transport and not a wheelie bin."

"Ladies and Gentlemen, we apologise for the delay, but there is a security alert at Victoria Station, and we are stuck here for the foreseeable future, so let's take our minds off it and pass some time together. All together now... 'Ten green bottles, hanging on a wall... '"

"I am sorry about the delay, apparently some nutter has just wandered into the tunnel at Euston. We don't know when we'll be moving again, but these people tend to come out pretty quickly... usually in bits."

"Ladies and Gentlemen, do you want the good news first or the bad news? The good news is that last Friday was my birthday and I hit the town and had a great time. I felt sadly let down by the fact that none of you sent me a card! I drive you to work and home each day and not even a card. The bad news is that there is a points failure somewhere between Stratford and East Ham, which means that we probably won't reach our destination for a good 90 minutes yet. We may have to stop and return. I won't reverse back up the line – simply get out, walk up the platform and go back to where we started. In the meantime, if you get bored you can simply talk to the man in front or behind you or opposite you. Let me start you off – Hi, my name's Gary, how do you do?"

"Please allow the doors to close. Try not to confuse this with 'please hold the doors open'. The two are distinct and separate instructions."

"May I remind all passengers that there is strictly no smoking allowed on any part of the Underground. However, if you are smoking a joint, it is only fair that you pass it round the rest of the carriage."

"Ladies and Gentlemen, I do apologise for the delay to your service. I know you're all dying to get home unless, of course, you happen to be married to my ex-wife, in which case you'll want to cross over to the westbound platform and go in the opposite direction."

"We are now travelling through Baker Street. As you can see, Baker Street is closed. It would have been nice if they had actually told me so I could tell you earlier but no, they don't think about things like that."

"Apparently this train is no longer terminating at Barking, but is in fact terminating here. I'm sorry about this, but I too was under the impression that this train was going to Barking, but 'they' have other ideas. I mean, why tell me? I'm merely the driver... "

"We can't move off because some c**t has their f*****g hand stuck in the door."

"Please note that the beeping noise coming from the doors means that the doors are about to close. It does not mean throw yourself or your bags into the doors."

"Your delay this evening is caused by the line controller suffering from elbow and backside syndrome, not knowing one from the other. I'll let you know any further information as soon as I'm given any."

"Hello, this is Dave speaking. I am the captain of your train, and we will be departing shortly. We will be cruising at an altitude of approximately zero feet, and our scheduled arrival time in Morden is 3:15 pm local time. The temperature in Morden is approximately 15 degrees Celsius, and Morden is in the same time zone as Mill Hill East, so there's no need to adjust your watches."

(On a delayed train to Epping, when the driver had a chat with a colleague, unaware he'd left the tannoy on): "Bollocks to the lot of them. I don't care if they don't make it to work."

"The train at platform three is not going to Parsons Green, but to Richmond. The train approaching platform two is also not going to Parsons Green, but to Ealing Broadway. These trains are not going to Parsons Green despite what the signalmen think."

"To the gentleman wearing the long grey coat trying to get on the second carriage, what part of 'stand clear of the doors' don't you understand?"

"Beggars are operating on this train; please do NOT encourage these professional beggars. If you have any spare change, please give it to a registered charity. Failing that, give it to me."

"Please let the passengers off the train first... Please let the passengers off the train first... Let the passengers off the train FIRST! Oh go on then – stuff yourselves in like sardines, see if I care – I'm going home."

Beware!

Warning on packet of peanuts: 'This product may contain nuts.'

Marks and Spencer's Bread Pudding: 'Product will be hot after heating.'

On a packet of crisps: 'You could be a winner! No purchase necessary. Details inside wrapper.'

Nabisco Easy Cheese: 'For best results, remove cap.'

On various sleeping aid medicines: 'Warning – may cause drowsiness.' (No, really?)

Frozen dinners: 'Serving suggestion – Defrost before eating.'

Printed on the bottom of tiramisu dessert: 'Do not turn upside down.'

On various food processors: 'Not to be used for the other use.' (Which is?)

On Boots' Children's Cough Medicine: 'Do not drive a car or operate machinery after taking this medication.'

Vacuum Cleaner: '1. Do not use to pick up gasoline or flammable liquids. 2. Do not use to pick up anything that is currently burning.'

On a bar of Palmolive soap: 'Directions – Use like regular soap.'

Rowenta Iron: Warning: 'Never iron clothes on the body.'

Swedish chainsaw: 'Do not attempt to stop chain with your hands or genitals.'

Electric rotary tool: 'This product not intended for use as a dental drill.'

Wheelbarrow: 'Do not use when temperature exceeds 140 degrees Fahrenheit.'

Bowl Fresh: 'Safe to use around pets and children, although it is not recommended that either be permitted to drink from toilet.'

500-piece jigsaw puzzle: 'Some assembly required.'

Mattress: 'Warning – do not attempt to swallow.'

Flying Goku: 'This label defies explanation. Take a look at the picture.'

Life-saving device: 'This is NOT a life-saving device!!!'

Child-sized Spiderman costume: 'Wearing this costume does not enable you to fly.'

Hair dryer: 'Do not use while sleeping.'

Hair colouring: 'Do not use as an ice cream topping.'

Harry Potter toy broom: 'This broom does not actually fly.'

Shop notice: Warning! Any complaints – tell it to the Rottweiler.'

Notice at London dock: 'Safety ladder – climb at your own risk.'

Road Signs

When this sign is under water, this road is impassable.

Stop – Drive Sideways.

Smile, You're On Radar.

Slow Cattle Crossing. No Overtaking For The Next 100 Years.

All signs converted to metric. Next sign 20 miles.

Danger Ahead.
Fasten Seatbelts And Remove Dentures.

Caution: Tree In Centre Of Road

Emergency Phone: 174 km Ahead

Trespassers Will Be Shot. **Survivors Will Be Shot Again.**

Stop! Exit Behind You.

Warning: Hitchhikers May Be Escaping Inmates.

No Parking Above This Sign

A Street: Downtown.
1¼ miles.
(Maybe they could have been more specific!)

Hair-raising Horoscopes

Taurus: You've got an exceptionally good rear ahead.

Gemini: Don't smell in the past.

Cancer: Don't look back at the future.

Virgo: You're going to get a second chance at a relationship you thought was rover.

Leo: A friend is going to fart from your life.

Libra: Don't get your knickers in a twist. Discard anything that holds you back.

Scorpio: Focus on who you are doing.

Sagittarius: Focus on new beginnings and sex for money.

Capricorn: As Uranus has been lodged in the same place for the last two years, this has caused you to be uptight. It will be defarting soon.

Aquarius: Trust in your slut feelings, especially with the opposite sex.

Pisces: As a pish sign, you're really dreamy.

Horoscope Line: For more star gazing tits, phone ******.

Horoscope Line: Phone calls to zodiac stars cost 60p per minute. Calls last approximately three years.

Crazy Ads

Experienced childminder available to take care of your child in my home. Fenced garden/play area, meals, and smacks included.

Wanted: Three-year-old teacher needed for pre-school. Experience preferred.

Missing: A purple lady's bicycle. Reward given.

Used cars: Why go anywhere else to be cheated? Come here first.

Dog for sale – eats anything and is fond of children.

Wanted: Woman to take care of child that does not smoke or drink.

For sale: Toys including Barfie doll. (Was the kid sick of it?)

Bed for sale: Excellent base. New mistress required as the old one is rather flat.

Auto Repair Service: Free pick-up and delivery. Try us once, you'll never go anywhere again.

Big Organ: Men – Increase the size of your organ by 1–3 feet (obviously they mean inches, or do they?)

Sewing machine repairs: We will oil your sewing machine and adjust tension in your home.

Advertisement in New York: Learn to read and speak English. Call us now.

Car sales garage: Parrot for sale. Was accepted as part exchange for a Ford car. Does not come with a warranty.

Sign in a laundry: Anyone leaving their laundry for more than 30 days will be disposed of.

Christmas sale: Lots of handmade gifts for the hard-to-find person.

Man seeks romance: Easy-going man seeks woman for romance. Must be pretty, slim, have a good sense of humour, like hiking, have long dark hair, blue eyes, nice smile, affectionate nature, non-smoker, enjoy eating in, and be as easy-going as I am.

Sign on window of dry cleaners: Drop your trousers here!

Sign in a laundry: **Automatic washing machines. Please remove all your clothes when the light goes out.**

Sign outside Italian laundry: Ladies, leave your clothes here and spend the day having a good time.

Sign outside builders: Our motto is to give customers the lowest possible prices and workmanship.

Sign outside new housing estate: We build houses that last. Underneath someone had written: 'I should hope so'.

Sign at garden centre: Nick your own strawberries.

Sign in front of a car wash: If you can't read this, it's time to wash your car.

Bikinis: Our bikinis are exciting. They are simply the tops.

Crazy Notices

Sign in department store: Bargain Basement Upstairs.

Sign in Copenhagen airline ticket office: We take your bags and send them in all directions.

Sign in Portuguese gift shop: English talking well. Speeching American too.

Sign on window of repair shop: We repair anything except – washing machines, hoovers, hair dryers, watches, clocks, refrigerators, lawn mowers, computers and televisions.

Sign outside second-hand shop: We exchange anything – bicycles, washing machines etc. Why not bring your wife along and get a wonderful bargain?

Sign in a Swedish hotel: Ladies are requested not to have children in the bar.

Sign at various military bases: Restricted to unauthorised personnel.

Sign in a New York restaurant: Customers who consider our waitresses uncivil ought to see the manager.

Swiss hotel menu: Today's Special – no ice cream.

Sign in a Japanese hotel: You are invited to take advantage of the chambermaid.

Sign in a Paris hotel: Please leave your values at the reception desk.

Sign in Acapulco hotel: The manager has personally passed all the water served here.

Sign in a hotel in Hawaii: The new swimming pool will be finished soon, as the contractors have thrown in the bulk of their workers.

Supermarket sign: Special offer – frozen dinners. Five for half-price (limit four).

Supermarket sign:
Special offer – Spaghetti hoops. Two tins for the price of three.

Church notice: On Easter Sunday we are pleased to announce that our chairwoman, Mrs Baxter, will come up and lay an egg on the altar.

Notice in a Los Angeles dance hall: Good clean dancing every night but Sunday.

Notice outside nightclub: We Are The Most Exclusive Nightclub In Town. Everyone Welcome.

Notice in factory: Fire alarm – in case of fire – run like anything!

Notice on the grounds of a public school: No trespassing without permission.

Notice outside new town hall: The Town Hall is closed until opening. It will remain closed after being opened. Open tomorrow.

Church notice: The Ladies' Circle have discarded all their clothes. They can be seen on Saturday in the Church Hall.

Bug off

A burger bar in Michigan was held up by a man at gunpoint who demanded the clerk hand over the money.
The clerk explained that the cash register wouldn't open unless a food order was processed. So the man ordered onion rings. The clerk said they weren't available on the breakfast menu. Frustrated, the man walked away!

Fast food in three days!

Employees at a computer company working late decided to order a fast-food delivery. Instead of phoning in the order, they thought that being computer guys, they'd order it via the Internet. They spent ages registering as new customers on the fast-food chain's web site. Finally, a message appeared on the screen. It said: 'Thank you for your business. You will be able to order food in three days.'

Give us a break!

A fast-food restaurant in America that had been open 24 hours every day for four years, decided to close on Christmas Day (for the first time ever). But they couldn't lock up because no one knew where the keys were.

Hookers

A North European government made plans to introduce a tax for prostitutes. Basically, the hookers would keep a calculator at the sides of their beds and total up the money clients paid them. This would allow the government to do to the girls what the girls have been doing to their customers for years.

Bees smell great

Bees know their stuff, according to one supermarket chain. They use bees to sniff strawberries to determine their ripeness. Apparently this works – so it's not to be sniffed at!

Fart mail

Workers at a Royal Mail sorting office in Somerset have been warned not to 'break wind' at work. Allegedly someone got wind of it and gave a 'kiss and smell' tip-off to the management.

Arrogant extra

A man was sent a bill from a New Zealand phone company. The bill included an extra charge to the man for being – 'an arrogant b*****d'.

Route beer

A computer-style wristwatch has been invented by beer lovers.
The watch shows the directions to the nearest pub. (As if they didn't know already.)

Poo plates

Hundreds of car number plates beginning with POO were recalled after the implications caused quite a stink!

Glueless

When a New Zealand town created its own special postage stamp, there was only one thing wrong with it. The sticky bit was on the wrong side of the stamp. The mistake, however, does make the stamps original.

In a pickle

An elderly woman couldn't get the top off her pickle jar and phoned the pickle helpline number. Somehow her wires got crossed, and she ended up talking to a sex chat line. (Bet they told her how to get her top off!)

Fish & hip hop

A fish and chip shop in Edinburgh has created a 'nightclub' atmosphere with flashing lights, mixing decks and music. (Troublemakers will be battered!)

Salt 'n' vinegar trips

Buses in Leicester are running on used fat from chip shops instead of diesel. It's better for the environment – and apparently it smells very tasty!

Well hung

A Norwegian landlord wants pictures of penises to decorate the walls of his pub. He believes that pubs are a male environment and thinks the penises are appropriate. (Okay, as long as they're well hung!)